Rivers

Margaret Slack

Mills & Boon
ON LOCATION
Book no. 6

Photographs by Alec Davis and the author
Drawings by Gareth Floyd; maps by Alec Davis

(Opposite) Scaleber Force, Yorkshire.
'Force' is a North Country word meaning
waterfall and if you travel round Yorkshire
you will find many waterfalls called forces

MILLS & BOON Limited, London

First published in Great Britain 1973
by Mills & Boon Limited, 17–19
Foley Street, London W1A 1DR.

© Margaret Slack 1973

ISBN 0 263 05312 1 (cased)
ISBN 0 263 05457 8 (limp)

Printed in Great Britain
by W & J Mackay Limited, Chatham
Bound by Hunter & Foulis,
Edinburgh

Contents

The sun evaporating seawater and turning
it into water vapour. On meeting cold air,
the vapour condenses and falls as rain

1 The water cycle

Have you ever watched a boiling kettle? The bubbling water rattles the lid and sends steam from the spout. If the kettle is left to boil for a long time, the kitchen windows become steamy and the walls wet. If you look carefully at the windows you will see small drops of water. This is because steam, which is a hot gas, turns to water when it meets a cold surface such as glass. If you breathe on a window the same thing happens. Your warm breath turns to water on meeting cold glass. The name for this is **condensation.**

If it is left long enough the kettle will boil dry. All the water will disappear even though you may not have taken any out. The name for this is **evaporation**. So, all the water in the kettle has turned to steam or water vapour because of the heat making it boil.

The sun, shining on the sea, evaporates some of the water. This becomes water vapour which, because it is a gas, rises. It becomes part of the air and moves along with it. On meeting a layer of cold air it condenses and falls on the earth as rain. Some of this rain stays on the surface of the earth,

where it evaporates. You will have noticed that after a shower of rain the pavements and roads very quickly become dry. This is because the rain is evaporated.

Now, not all the rain disappears in this way. Some soaks into the ground where it is used by the roots of plants. Some seeps into cracks in the ground. The rest runs along the surface of the ground and joins rivers.

Underneath the soil there is rock. There are various types, because thousands of millions of years ago the earth was built up from layers of rock. Some of these rocks absorb water. That is, they soak it up just as a piece of blotting paper soaks up ink. Sandstone is like this. Other types of rock, for example limestone, have cracks through which the water runs. Rocks that admit water are known as **pervious** rocks. As the water passes downwards it will in time reach a layer of rock through which it cannot pass. This is **impervious** rock. It will find its way along this until it reaches a point where the impervious rock meets pervious rock. When this takes place at the surface of the earth the water comes out as a

What happens to the rain

RAIN

RE·VAPORISED DIRECT

UNDERGROUND WATER

SURFACE RUN-OFF

Rain seeps into lines of weakness in rock

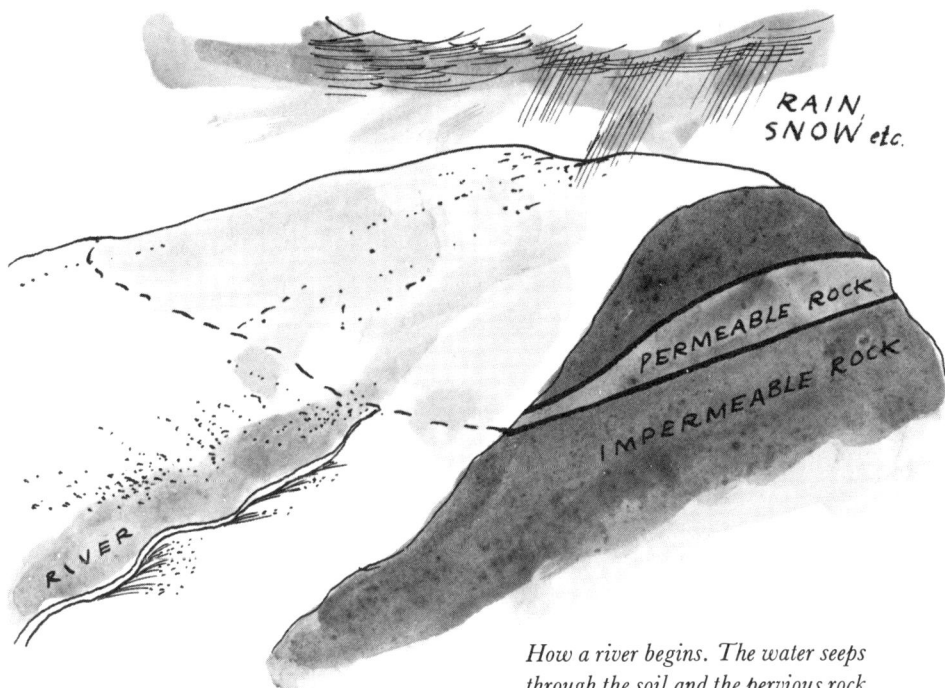

How a river begins. The water seeps through the soil and the pervious rock until it reaches the impervious rock where it emerges as a spring

spring. This spring is the beginning of a **river**. Water always flows downhill, never uphill. In time all rivers reach the sea where the sun evaporates the sea water and the whole story begins again. This story is known as a **water cycle**.

The source of the River Wharfe, Yorkshire

The second stage (called youth) of the River Wharfe

2 The story of a river

There are four stages in the life story of a river, and during each it behaves in a particular way. At first the water flows very slowly, carrying along small twigs or bits of loose soil. After a mile or two it begins to travel more swiftly. More water has reached it from small tributary streams. It has picked up tiny pebbles and scraps of soil as it has travelled. This second stage of the river is called **youth**. Like most young people it has plenty of energy, flowing fast and splashing over rocks.

Swiftly moving water has a great power to wear away. As the river moves it carries along large and small stones, sand and clay. This material increases its power to wear away. Not only are the banks worn but also the floor, which is called the **river bed**. The river makes a valley shaped like a letter V.

Swiftly moving water can cut through rock and carry large boulders downstream

When a river cuts a V-shaped
valley, you will notice jutting-out bits
of land that seem to fit together.
These 'jutting-out bits' are called
spurs. Because they fit, or interlock,
like the fingers of your hands when
you clasp them, they are known as
interlocking spurs.

Here are two illustrations that show
you the energy of a river. There is
foam, froth and swirling water. After
days of heavy rain there is even more
foam, froth and swirling water. We
say then that the river is in **spate**. If
there is not a great deal of water, **rock
pools** are formed as in the illustra-
tion on page 15

Interlocking spurs

*The River Wharfe in spate under Burnsall
Bridge (Above opposite)*

*The River Wye flooding at Brockweir,
Gloucestershire (Below opposite)*

Moving water with a much stronger current in midstream

If you look carefully at the picture opposite you will see that it shows moving water. Can you see that the water moves more swiftly in one part of the river than the other?

As the stones in the water are whirled round they bump into each other. This wears them away so that they become smooth and round. As they whirl they wear round holes in the rocky bed of the river that can be seen when there is not a great deal of water.

As boulders are whirled round by swiftly moving water they gouge round holes in the river bottom

The Strid – a channel only a few feet wide but very deep – on the River Wharfe

In this picture the river races through a narrow channel it has cut through the rock. The water has worn away the rocks underneath those we can see here. The channel through which the water flows is so narrow – its name is the Strid – that people are tempted to try to jump across. Few succeed, and those who fail will fall into the raging torrent and their bodies swirl from side to side under the rocks.

You may also find **waterfalls** in the second stage of a river. As we saw in Chapter 1 there are different layers of rock making up the earth. Some absorb water, some do not. Some are hard, others soft. We have also seen the power of water to wear away rock. Soft rock is worn away much faster than hard rock, so pieces of hard rock are left protruding (or sticking out) and the water flows over them, making a waterfall. Where there are several strips of hard rock, a series of small waterfalls, or **rapids**, is formed. Fast-flowing water also cuts a deep **gorge** in rock. In such a gorge the river cuts back and so makes a water-fall.

A

B

C

Three ways in which a waterfall can be formed. The black areas represent hard rock that water cannot wear away as quickly as soft

The waterfalls on the following four pages are:
Thornton Force, Yorkshire. The water falls 40 feet into a deep pool

Pecca Falls near Ingleton, Yorkshire

Scaleber Force, Yorkshire

Gordale Beck runs through a deep gorge known as Gordale Scar, where the cliffs rise to over 300 feet on each side, to join the River Aire

A dredger
By courtesy of the Port of London Authority

In time the energy of the river seems to become less. In its middle stage it moves more slowly and does not carry so heavy a load. But the energy is still great because there is now much more water. First the heavy stones are dropped. But the river still carries sand and mud – this is the **silt** that, when dropped later, fills up the river so that **dredging** is needed. In this stage the main work of the river is transportation or carrying, and stones are rolled along the river bed. The valley becomes wider and more open.

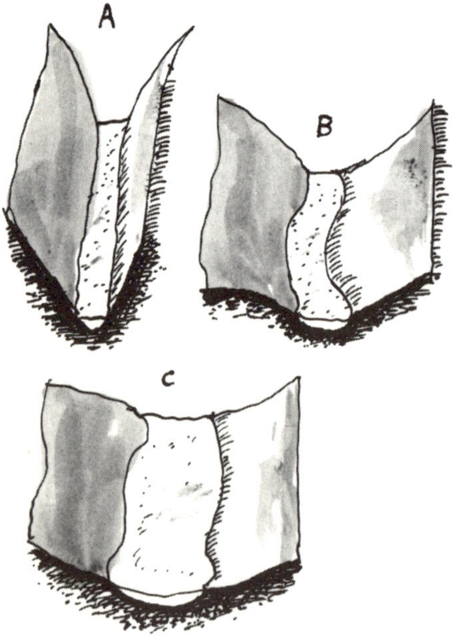

The valley of a river widens as it descends from hilly districts (A) to the sea (C)

LONG REACH

A meandering river

In the last stage of the river, the valley widens. Here the river has not a great deal of energy and wanders, or **meanders**, lazily across a plain. Now its main work is **deposition**. That is it deposits, or lays down, a great deal of what is being carried.

When flooding takes place mud is spread over the ground. In England this is suitable for growing grass. (When the River Nile floods in Egypt, the rich mud enables many crops to be grown.) But of course not everyone is a farmer, so, if people do not want rivers to flood, the river banks are strengthened. By bringing down mud, a river can raise the height of its floor or river bed and also raise its banks.

The amount of mud brought down by a river is quite amazing. The River Thames (where the amount is not really very big), brings down – floating in the water – about a quarter of a million tons every year. This equals one ton every minute.

Although this is the typical life story of a river, not all rivers are exactly like this. In mountainous districts some rivers flow directly into the sea. Other rivers, for example the Thames, do not flow through mountains.

We have now found the most important things to discover about rivers. But by using our eyes carefully and spending some time we can find out much more.

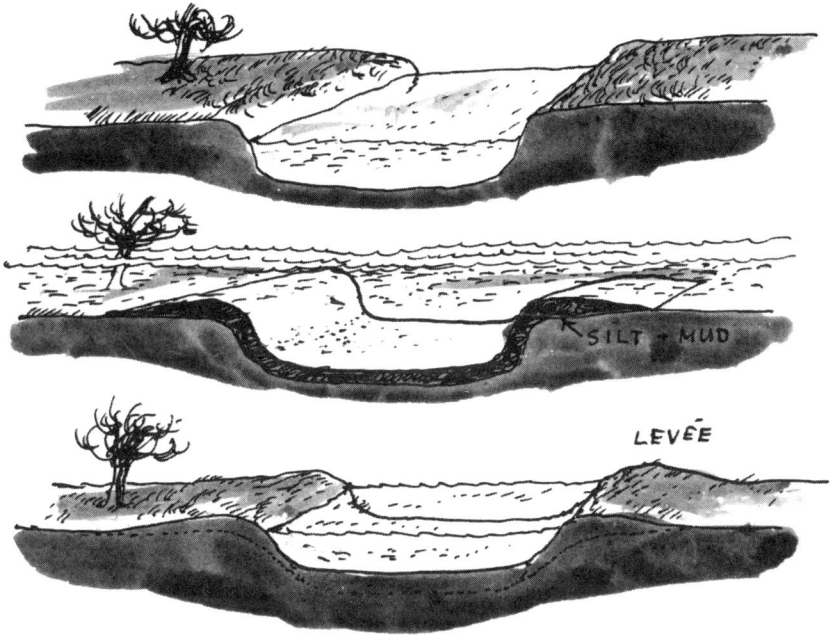

SILT + MUD

LEVÉE

How raised river banks (known as levées)
are formed. When a river floods (middle
drawing) it deposits layers of mud and silt
on the banks. In time these become covered
with grass and so form new raised banks

The estuary of a river

Notice the various sizes of potholes made by the stones as they are swirled round by the water. Can you see the way in which the rocks have been cut?

Notice, too, that the river leaves large stones even in its early stages.

By looking very carefully you can see a pattern about this. The large stones seem to be towards the middle of the river with the stones gradually getting smaller towards the edge. Can you suggest a reason for this?

A river wears away its banks. Sometimes it wears one bank more than another. Do they overhang? Can you see any roots sticking out like a giant's whiskers, from the soil?

(*Author's photographs*)

Can you see any places along the river bank where the river seems to have altered its course slightly?

What shape are the stones in the river bed? Are they round and smooth? Are they flat, narrow and with jagged edges?

Can you find a tree growing on the river bank very close to the water? Or can you see a large boulder or tree trunk in the water? Does this trap twigs and leaves floating downstream?

If you look at a river in the early
stages you may find a floodgate like
the one above. It is not a bridge. Can
you suggest its purpose?

Here is a flood indicator. In time of
very heavy rain it shows the speed at
which the river is rising.

If you live in parts of the North of
England you will know that fields
have stone walls round them rather
than hedges or fences.

Below are two pictures of stone walls. Can you see a difference between the stones that were used? One was near a river, the other a long way away. Which wall do you think was near the river?

In the early stages of a river the water is clear. Look carefully at it. Is it brown from the peat on the moors? (see the picture on the back cover of this book). Does it reflect the colour of the stone? Perhaps it is greeny blue. Is it in fact unpolluted? Careless people who spend weekends in the country sometimes use rivers and streams as dumping grounds for rubbish. Can you see any tins or bottles in the river?

What is the name of your river? Many river names are very old, dating from before the Romans came here. Many got their names from words meaning water, or from words that describe water. **Avon** was a British word meaning river (any river). **Isca** was another British word meaning water. One way of learning a foreign language is to learn the names of simple objects. The teacher holds things in front of a class and repeats their names over and over again. When we have difficulty in a foreign country we can point to what we want. The name of the object is stated as the person hands it to us. Now when early invaders came they pointed to a river, or water and were told 'avon' or 'isca'. The general name then became the particular name. There are river Avons in several counties. The rivers Exe, Usk, and Esk, are all variants of the word 'isca'. Some names of rivers describe the river – winding one, flowing one bubbling one. Think of a name for your local bit of river.

3 Using rivers

Coracles (known as curraghs in Ireland) were small round boats made of leather stretched round a wicker framework. They are still used in parts of Wales and Ireland

From the earliest days of history people have made use of rivers. No doubt men caught fish in them in the Old Stone Age. Later on, when men had learnt how to make boats they fished from these. When they had caught all the fish they could in one part of the river they would move to another, carrying their light-weight boats on their backs.

The Angles and Saxons who came from North Germany in the fifth, sixth and seventh centuries, that is from about AD 400–700, used the rivers that flow into the North Sea to sail as far inland as possible. Later, in the ninth century, the Vikings who came from Denmark and Norway used these rivers for the same purpose. At first these invaders came to raid and to explore. Later they came to stay.

The Saxon word for homestead is **ham** and for homestead with a fence round it the word is **ton. By** is a Viking word for village and **thorp** for farm or hamlet. If there are places with these endings in your river valley, it is likely that they were first settled by Saxons or Vikings. If you would like to find out more about this, use the volumes of the English Place Name Society. These books are available in public libraries and there is a separate volume for most of the counties in England.

Having decided to settle, they would look round for somewhere suitable to build houses. They would need a place fairly near water but not near enough to be flooded if there was heavy rain. They would choose ground that was high enough to be dry but not so high that it was cold and windy. They needed, too, a place in which the soil was light enough to plough and grow crops. No doubt many such places would be in river valleys and it was here that they

built their houses and villages. When they visited neighbours further along the valley they would find the easiest way. They would then tell their fellow villagers who later used the same route and so on. In time a footpath was made along the riverside.

Have you seen any castles near rivers? Castles often _were_ built near rivers. One way in which they could get rid of their sewage was to let it flow straight into the river. So you see even in the Middle Ages there was pollution. Why wasn't pollution then such a problem as it is now? If you think hard you can find at least two reasons. But getting rid of sewage was not the most important reason for putting castles near water. What was it?

Since these days men have continued to use rivers. Overleaf is a diagram showing the use of water by the industries in a city. The diagram does not refer to any particular river and covers many centuries of industry. Notice that the **brewing industry** was near the beginning of the river where the water was clean. The **corn mills** which needed swiftly running water to turn the mill wheels were also near the beginning of the river (that is in the hills).

Near the meadows where the sheep grazed were the weaving sheds and **fulling** mills. Soft water was needed to wash the fleeces of the sheep before the wool was woven. **Soft** water

BREWING

CORN MILLS

CITY

MARKET

SLAUGHTER-HOUSE

CORNLANDS

SKINNERS

WEAVING & FULLING SHEDS

BONE YARD

LEATHER VATS

SHEEP GRAZE

HORN WORKS

WOOL DRESSING (TALLOW)

GLUE BOILERS

SOAP BOILERS

CHANDLERS

REFUSE

BEES WAX

REFUSE DUMPS

FRUIT & VEGETABLES

FLAX

POTASH PITS

BUILDING & BASKET WILLOWS

SMALL FISHING BOATYARDS

HEMP

FLOW

WASTE WOOD - TAR

RETTING PONDS

FISH SMOKING & CURING SHEDS

ROPE WORKS

THATCH REEDS

WILD FOWL

SALTINGS

ESTUARY

How industries use the river   *The water mill at Skenfrith, Monmouth-*
                                        shire . . .

. . . and the water wheel in close up

lathers easily; **hard** water does not.
You remember that we spoke of the
water cycle in the first chapter?
When it leaves the clouds rain is pure
like water that has been boiled. On
its way through the atmosphere it
absorbs carbon dioxide, a gas, which
gives it an acid quality. The rain
finds its way into the cracks of rocks
and gradually wears the rock away
making the cracks wider. But the
weak acid in it also dissolves some
types of rock, for example limestone,
and makes the cracks still bigger. So
water that comes from limestone
rock, or that which contains lime,
such as chalk, is hard because it has
absorbed lime. Derbyshire water is
hard. If you live in an area of hard
water perhaps you will have noticed
that a coating of white lime gradually
collects inside the kettle. The weak
acid in rain water has no such effect
on some rocks, such as millstone grit.
Water that comes from such rocks is
soft.

Now this can have an effect a long way away. Big cities collect their water from mountainous areas scores of miles away. Manchester gets much of its water from the Lake District, Birmingham from mid-Wales. So, depending on where a city's water comes from, it is either hard or soft.

Water is collected in a **dam** and then sent by pipeline to towns. A natural lake can be made into a dam. Or an artificial lake is made by damming, or making a barrier across a stream or river. This is something you can look out for. Of course the first workers in the woollen industry did not have this information about hard and soft water. They discovered by trial and error which was the most suitable for washing wool. Where does the water in your tap begin?

You can find bits of wool from the shaggy fleece of the sheep on hedges and fences and sharp edges of stone walls. If you do find any take it home and wash it in warm soapy water. When it is dry pull it out carefully into a long thread and twist it as you pull. This is how the first spinners learnt their craft. They speeded up the process by twisting a wooden stick or spindle in a whorl – a round piece of stone with a hole in. The wool was pulled out with the fingers and the long thread wound onto the spindle.

Swiftly flowing water was needed to turn the wheels that operated the fulling mills. **Fulling** is a process in the woollen industry in which the cloth is soaked in soapy water and beaten with very heavy wooden

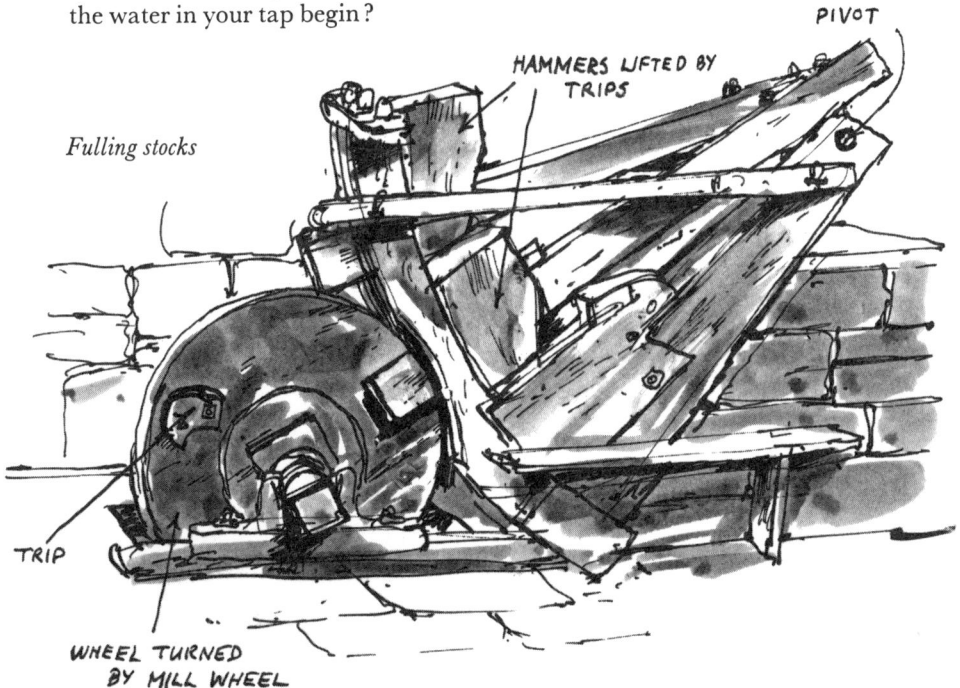

Fulling stocks

PIVOT

HAMMERS LIFTED BY TRIPS

TRIP

WHEEL TURNED BY MILL WHEEL

hammers called mallets. This is to
clean and shrink the cloth – after all
no one wants to wear a coat that will
shrink the first time it gets wet. At
first, this beating of the cloth was
done by human beings treading on it.
(This is where the surname Walker
comes from.) In the thirteenth
century mills were built and the
mallets worked by water power.

To describe someone by his occupation, e.g., Walker, is one way in which
surnames began. There are other
occupational names such as Dyer,
Fuller, Baker, Miller. Another way
of identifying someone is to describe
where he or she lives. Names such as
Thomas at the Bridge, Peter of the
Dike, Matilda of Ripplingham, which
are found in documents of the Middle
Ages, are very awkward. But East-
wood and Greenwood probably
began like this. Some people were
described by what they looked like
(appearance), or by what they *were*
like (character). Names like Broad-
head and Whitehead, Slack and
Good, probably began in this way.
To say that someone is the son of
someone was a simple way of identifying a person. In this way names
like Johnson, Thompson and Robin-
son began. Would this last method be
very practical now? Perhaps you
could make a list of the surnames of

*The Dinas dam, part of the Rheidol hydro-
electric scheme in Wales. By courtesy of
the Central Electricity Generating Board*

members of your class, your school or
your street. Arrange them in columns
showing the different types of name.
If you visit another part of the British
Isles see if you can find names that
differ from those in your own district. Look carefully at names on
shops.

Lower down stream from the fulling
there was farmland on which fruit
and vegetables were grown. Further
on still flax and hemp grew. Water is
needed for **retting** or soaking the
flax and hemp. This process dissolves
the sticky material on the fibres of the
flax stem so that they can be made
into linen. In the case of hemp
retting soaks off the outer husk or
shell. The liquid resulting from hemp

retting is nasty, brown and harmful
to cattle. But hemp was very neces-
sary because from it ropes and ships'
sails were made.

Willows grew in this area too. These
were important for baskets and long
straight poles suitable for fences.
The candle makers needed grease
which they obtained from the wool
dressers and from the bees just across
the river. In days before sugar was
cheap and plentiful bees were kept
and the honey used for sweetening.
Beeswax (which made the honey-
comb) and tallow (animal fat) also
supplied the soap boilers.

Until the nineteenth century, when there were many railways, animals were driven to market by drovers who walked with them and drove them along the grassy lanes to market. The animals fed on their journey from grass at the wayside and drank water from streams. It was sensible that the **tanners**, or makers of leather, should be near the cattle market so that they could obtain the skins from the cattle when they had been slaughtered. The tanners needed bark from the oak tree or willow strippings to preserve the skins. They also needed water to fill the tanks in which the hides soaked in lime water to remove the hairs. The horn workers, who made kitchen and table dishes from the horns of animals, and glue boilers, also needed water.

But perhaps the most important use of rivers was for **transport**. Most rivers, except for the very smallest streams, were used for boats that were towed (pulled by men or horses) or sailed along. In the Middle Ages the monks of Yorkshire, who kept thousands of sheep and made a great deal of money from the sale of wool, sent it out of England by way of the Ouse and Humber rivers. Stone, from which York Minster and Ely Cathedral were built, was also carried by river.

There were rules and regulations about building mills and bridges. They could not to be built in places where they would get in the way of boats. All the same, boatmen were obstructed by other users of rivers. Corn millers built dams to provide water to turn the water wheels. Fishermen built weirs to trap fish. Sometimes barge owners had to wait hours or even days until the miller agreed to move some of the timber from his weir so that there was enough water to allow a barge to sail.

Sometimes rivers flooded, sometimes in dry weather there was not sufficient water for a boat to sail. All the same, a great many of the rivers were used to carry goods. Coal was brought along the **tributaries** (small rivers joining the main one) of the Severn. Salt was brought from Droitwich.

The rivers suffered from **silting**. This means that so much sand and mud was carried by the river from the hills that lower down there was a danger that the river would become blocked. This was made worse because in order to make their loads lighter the bargemen used to throw their ballast overboard. **Ballast** is anything heavy that is carried in a ship to make sure she is heavy enough to be able to sail. An empty ship sailing to collect goods would need ballast. On her return, when she was laden with goods she would not need ballast.

During the eighteenth century the number of people living in England grew larger. There was a need to improve the rivers so that they would

The more important rivers of the British Isles

NARROW NECK OF LAND   CUT-OFF   OX·BOW LAKE

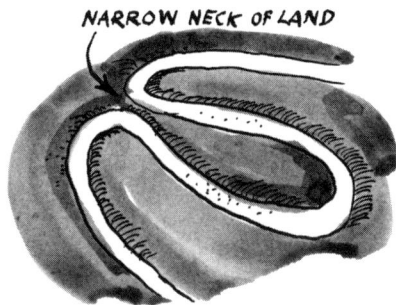

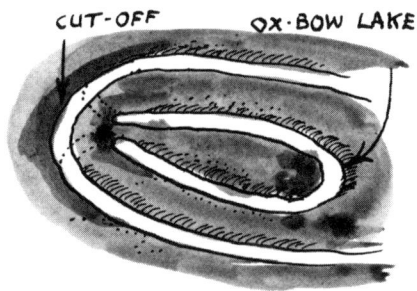

*Formation of ox-bow lake on a sharply
meandering river*

be more efficient as a means of transport. Weirs were removed so that it was easier for boats to sail. River banks were strengthened. In some places where rivers had meandered a great deal, cuts were made. These cuts were small channels filled with water and joined two sections of a river by cutting across a meander.

Cutting small channels for water gave people the idea of cutting big ones – **canals**. These were made mostly in the North of England and in the Midlands. This was because it was here that the numbers of people had increased most. Canals were cut here also because there was more industry in the North of England and the Midlands than anywhere else. Efficient transport was needed to bring raw material to the factories and to take goods away again.

Canals were more useful than rivers. They did not become blocked with silt. People were able to control the amount of water going into them. They did not dry up or flood.

The opening of the Stockton to Darlington Railway in 1825 and of the Liverpool to Manchester Railway in 1830 led to the spread of railways throughout the country. This meant that many of the goods carried by canal and river were now taken by rail. There is a book about railways in this series that will tell you more. Later, in the twentieth century, old bridle tracks and footpaths along the valleys were made into roads, roads used by motor traffic.

Canals, railways and roads were built along the valley bottom, using the easiest route. This is the route made by the river. So you will often find that in a broad valley the river, railway, road and canal run alongside each other.

Fishing is a sport that uses rivers. Another name for fishing is **angling**, and clubs for fishermen are angling clubs. Often stretches of river are used by certain angling clubs and people who are not members of that club are not allowed to fish there.

A typical fishing river

Shrimping at low tide in the Severn Estuary

The arms on Fishmongers' Hall, London. The Fishmongers' Company is one of the twelve great livery companies of the City of London whose first charter was granted by Edward I in 1272. The Company's officials can still examine the fish offered for sale in Billingsgate Market

Can you see any such notices? They may have the letters AA, standing for Angling Association on them. BAA might mean Bolton Angling Association. Where are the headquarters of the angling association? Is it a town near that river or is it many miles away?

Ships are built along rivers such as the Clyde and the Tyne. Not all rivers are suitable for this. I wonder if you can think of the reason? You will have to think of the sea, shelter and deep water. Rivers that were once suitable are no longer so. What is the reason for this? Buckler's Hard in Hampshire, where many of the ships for Nelson's navy were built, is situated near land that was well wooded. The Tyne and Clyde are situated near coalfields.

Buckler's Hard, Hampshire. The village was built in the late eighteenth century and was intended as a harbour but became an important shipbuilding centre. It is little more than a terraced street running down to the Beaulieu River. The last house in the terrace was the Master Builder's House, now a hotel. There is also a maritime museum here

Littlehampton Harbour is on a river estuary. Note the swing bridge

4 Bridges and boats

The early settlers who built their houses and villages near rivers would in time wish to cross the river and so they looked for suitable crossing places. A narrow stretch of river with shallow water would be the most suitable. No doubt at first they paddled through and, when they became tired of getting wet feet, would throw in a big flat stone – and then another, and another, so forming **stepping stones**.

A shallow place was also used as a **ford** where carts or animals could cross the river. Many town and village names end in the word 'ford', even though the stream or river was later crossed by a bridge. Ford names are interesting. Some describe the colour of the water, or the length or width of the ford. In other places the ford gets its name from some important person who lived nearby, or from trees or flowers that grew there. Perhaps you could collect names of towns and villages in which there is the word 'ford'. The English Place Name Society books will help.

Another way to cross was to build a **bridge**. Very early in time men discovered that the simplest way to do this was to find a thick tree, cut it

A ford near Bolton Abbey, Yorkshire

down and put it across the river. Or better still they would find a tree growing on the river bank so that if it was chopped down it would fall across the water. Two trunks side by side with logs between would enable a man to push a cart across. Men who lived in forests plaited ropes and slung them between trees on each side of the river. They would then cross like monkeys, or as you do in the gymnasium. If there were two ropes men could walk on one and use the other as a handrail. Can you see how the two types of bridge shown opposite have grown from these ideas?

(Above opposite)
A wooden bridge near Ingleton, Yorkshire

(Below opposite)
Albert Bridge, London, built in 1873

Single-arched stone bridge (now buttressed as support against traffic) in Clapham, Yorkshire

Waterloo Bridge, London

Another way of building a bridge was to make an **arch**. To do this a framework of wood was made across the river. Then, wedge-shaped pieces of stone named **voussoirs** were built side by side in a curve. When the last piece at the crown of the arch was pushed into place the wood framework could be taken away. Each piece of stone pushed hard against the one just below it until all the weight was transferred to the ground at the ends of the arch. When the main arch was formed the space above could be filled in with stones or bricks. But by watching the water and the way it behaved, men learned how to make other bridges.

If a tree or big stone falls into a river the stones, twigs and leaves brought down by the water pile up in front of it. Men used the knowledge that they had gained by looking when they started to build weirs or bridges. They would put a line of thin branches across the river. These would have enough space to let the water pass through, but the rubbish would pile up in front. They would carry out stones to add to the debris and soon a barrier would be built.

If a bridge with more than one arch was needed, stones were carried out in baskets, so that a series of barriers was built in the water. One way of

Clapper bridge, Malham, Yorkshire

joining these barriers was to stretch
large slabs of stone between them.
This was known as a **clapper
bridge**.

Men eventually developed these piles
of stones into pillars known as **piers**.
It was discovered that if angles were
built on these they served two pur-
poses. In the water they lessened the
pressure of the water on the piers, so
making wear and tear on them less.
On the road they made alcoves in
which people could stand to let
traffic pass.

Bridge building was thought of as a
religious duty, done for the good of
people in general. At the same time it
was a money-making affair. Small
packhorse bridges were probably
paid for by pedlars who travelled
about the countryside selling goods to
remote farms; or drovers who drove
animals to market. Many people who
built bridges charged those who used
them. Sometimes a chapel was built on
a bridge so that travellers could pray
for a safe journey. But even in the

Bridge with piers, Ilkley, Yorkshire

Alcove on Burnsall Bridge, Yorkshire

Packhorse bridge, Clapham, Yorkshire

Bridge with piers, Bingley, Yorkshire

Fourteenth-century chantry chapel of St Mary (one of four bridge chapels remaining in England) over the River Calder in Wakefield, Yorkshire

chapels there was a small room for the bridge-keeper to watch for travellers so that he could charge them a fee.

Of course bridge building has continued since the Middle Ages. In some cases old bridges have not been sufficient to cope with modern traffic. In these cases another bridge has been built by the side of the old one. Metal has also been used for bridge building.

Look carefully at any bridges there are. Are they in good repair? If not, it is probable that they are not used a great deal. Can you find any piles of stones or bits of metal on the river bank? This may mean that once there was a bridge there that has now been washed away.

Can you see a date on a bridge? Perhaps the bridge has been built in memory of someone, in which case there will probably be a notice to say so. Perhaps the iron railings on the bridge have been decorated. Those on one of the big bridges in York have been decorated with the white rose emblem. This is the emblem of Yorkshire.

Many bridges have on them the mark, a sort of trade mark, of the mason who built them. You will have to look

An old and modern bridge side by side in Gordale, Yorkshire

very carefully for these. Sometimes
they are on the parapet, or edge, of
the bridge. Sometimes they are underneath. If there is not a great deal of
water in the river you can get right to
the edge and underneath the bridge.
The mark of the mason may be his
initials like these, from Airton in
Yorkshire, WM WTIH. Collect masons'
marks in your district. You may find
that more than one bridge was built
by the same mason.

You may have noticed that many
modern bridges are graceful and well
designed. Some bridge builders have
become famous. Try to find out the
name of the person who built the
bridge that interests you. If you

would like to find out more about
him there is a series of volumes that
will help you. This is *The Dictionary of
National Biography*, and you will find
it in the public library.

Have a good look at a big bridge. Is
it wide enough to carry the amount
of traffic? Are there big queues of
traffic at rush-hour time? Why was
the bridge built just there and not a
mile or two away? Why was it more
sensible to build a bridge at all
rather than a tunnel?

The method of trapping twigs and
leaves that was used to form the
foundation of bridges was also used
to make **weirs**. A few thin branches

The new London Bridge (opened March 1973) under construction. The old bridge was dismantled stone by stone and shipped over to America.

A weir at Wakefield, Yorkshire

or hurdles were put across the river. These collected the stones, twigs and leaves that had floated downstream. When built the weir trapped water so that above it there was a stretch of fairly deep water that was useful to fishermen. Water was also trapped for use by mill owners. At the weir the water was directed into a narrow channel in which there was a water wheel. So, wherever there is a weir you may be sure there is, or has been, a mill.

Of course it was not always possible to build a bridge across a river. In this case **ferry boats** were used.

Ferries were common in the Middle Ages. People valued the right to operate a ferry as in this way they could make money. But it was also dangerous. Imagine that you were a ferryman and a runaway thief or murderer made you take him across the river threatening you with harm if you refused!

There are fewer ferries now than there were. The largest ferry system in Britain is that which crosses the River Mersey. If a route across a river is short and likely to be busy, a ferry that is easy to move and turn is needed. A **paddle-wheel ferry** is

Ballachulish Ferry, Scotland

*The Hythe to Southampton ferry has a pier
to reach the deeper water and a tiny railway
to reach the end of the pier*

then the most suitable. Some ferries however have to cross rivers where currents are strong. It is important that the ferry should not be swept away if its engines fail. In this case a **chain ferry** is most suitable. A chain across the river bed is fastened firmly on each bank. This is looped round a sprocket (a sort of knob on the edge of the wheel), which is driven by the engines. The boat is guided across as it picks up the chain.

Another type of ferry is a **transporter**. This is very suitable for use over a narrow span of water. It must be high so that it does not get in the way of shipping. The transporter is worked by electric power. Have you seen any of these types of ferry? Do you think they are suitable for the type of river they cross? Is there a ferry on your local river, or a road called Ferry Road where you live?

Other types of boats and ships used, and still use, rivers. Can you see boats like these on your rivers?

Racing boat

Canoe

A pleasure boat on the Thames seen in front of HMS Belfast, now a floating museum

Hydrofoil

Lighters or barges

*Thames River Police launch. By permission
of the Commissioner of Police, New
Scotland Yard*

Are there any cargo boats, and any
passenger boats? What sort of cargo
is carried? Where do the ships come
from? The port where they are
registered is usually painted on the
ship near the name. If there are ships
in the river there will probably be
cranes too. Why are they there?

River buoy

Can you see anything like this in the
middle of the river? At the top there
is a flashing light. Can you guess its
purpose? Are there any mills and
factories along the river bank? Are
they still in use? What do they make?

5 Potholes and water sinks

Just as people behave in odd and un-usual ways, so too do rivers. We learned earlier how some rivers are born – through a join between im-pervious and pervious rock. (Rivers also rise on impervious rock.) Rivers disappear when the opposite happens, when pervious meets impervious rock. Limestone is a rock that has many cracks. We learned on page 36 that acid in rainwater dissolves the stone and widens the cracks. A river trickling into and through these cracks makes them wider still.

The point at which the river dis-appears is called a **water sink** or **swallow hole**. Eventually large underground holes are made in the limestone. Our river flows into one of these and in time pops out again when a layer of impervious rock is reached. These underground holes and passages are known as **potholes**. One of the most famous is Gaping Gill on the slopes of the mountain Ingleborough. Underneath the mountain, this and other rivers have worn miles and miles of passages and large holes.

Gaping Gill

(*Opposite*)

'*The Hall of Wookey*' – *just one of the caverns that can be visited in the Wookey Hole Caves (where the River Axe runs underground) in the Mendip Hills*

Drops of water leaking in through the roof of a large hole such as this leave tiny grains of limestone behind. As each drop leaves more grains to be added to the first lot, 'stone icicles' are formed hanging down from the roof. The name for these is **stalactites**. Drops of water falling to the floor of the cave behave in the same way. The 'icicles' grow upwards and are known as **stalagmites**. The making of caves and 'icicles' takes millions of years.

Gaping Gill is a deep hole having a single drop of nearly 400 feet. There are many potholes that are deeper, but they descend bit by bit. Exploring these potholes is an interesting, exciting and dangerous occupation, even though maps have been made showing the passages in many potholes. To get into them people need special equipment such as rope ladders, climbing ropes and miners' helmets with powerful lamps. Crawling in muddy passages can be exciting, but if there is heavy rain when people are in a pothole they can be in great danger. In this case the river, fast-flowing because of the rain, can flood the hole, drowning anyone in it.

Diagram of Gaping Gill

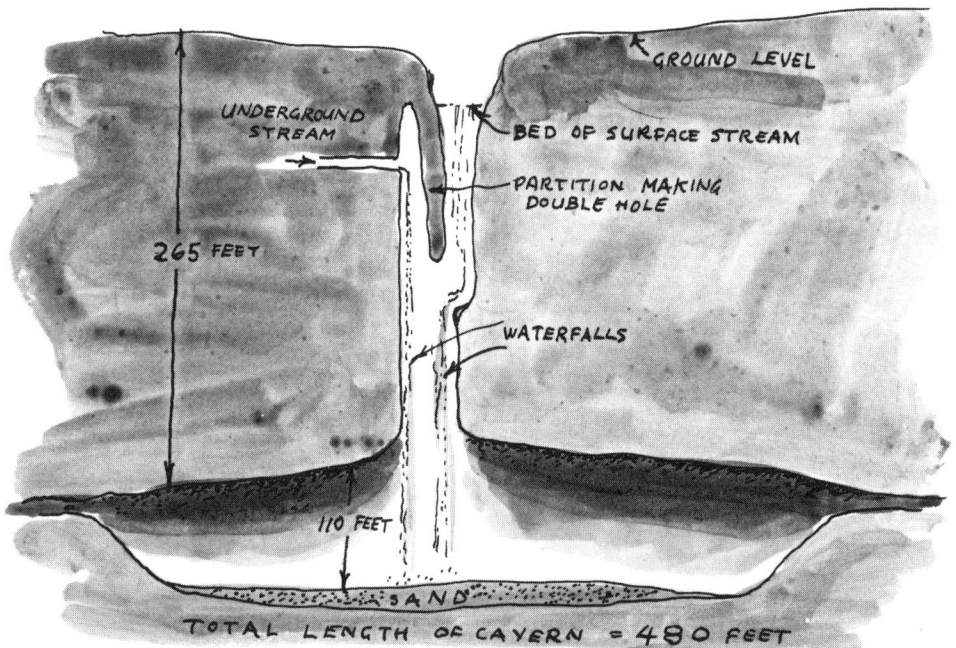

GROUND LEVEL

UNDERGROUND STREAM

BED OF SURFACE STREAM

PARTITION MAKING DOUBLE HOLE

265 FEET

WATERFALLS

110 FEET

SAND

TOTAL LENGTH OF CAVERN = 480 FEET

Gaping Gill needs a winch and gantry to lower people into it. Sitting in a bosun's chair wrapped in oilskins, one is lowered through the waterfall down, down, almost touching the edge of the rock as one travels. Once down there is a large space, or chamber as it is known. This even has a telephone connecting it with the surface. The main chamber is big enough to fit a cathedral inside and still leave spare room.

The drawing below shows another point at which a river disappears – the Water Sinks at Malham. For years people thought that the Cove was the place where the water re-appeared. Then they began to have doubts. A 'dig' was started near the Water Sinks to try to get into the underground passage people were sure lay between the Sinks and the Cove. Divers tried to get underneath the Cove to the cave they thought lay behind it. Then coloured dyes were put into the water. It was found that the stream at the Cove had disappeared, not at the sinks, but elsewhere. The water going under-ground at the sinks reappeared at another point.

Water Sinks above Malham Cove, York-shire

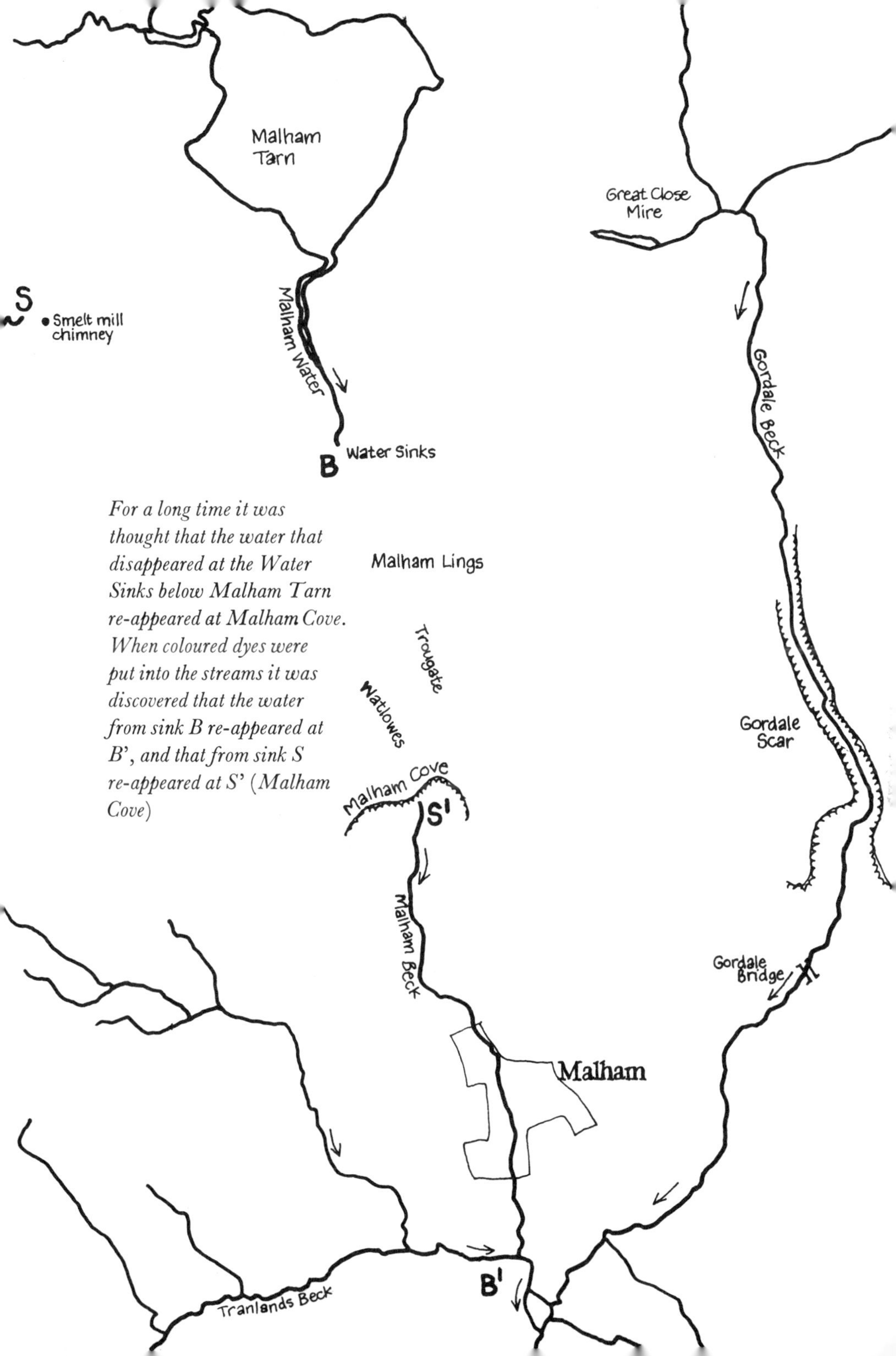

Malham Tarn

S
• Smelt mill chimney

Malham Water

B Water Sinks

For a long time it was thought that the water that disappeared at the Water Sinks below Malham Tarn re-appeared at Malham Cove. When coloured dyes were put into the streams it was discovered that the water from sink B re-appeared at B', and that from sink S re-appeared at S' (Malham Cove)

Malham Lings

Trougate

Watlowes

Malham Cove

S'

Malham Beck

Great Close Mire

Gordale Beck

Gordale Scar

Gordale Bridge

Malham

Tranlands Beck

B'

Malham Cove with a curving wall of solid
limestone that is nearly 300 feet high

6 Lost rivers and bores

There are many lost rivers of another sort. Cities have been built over rivers. One is Bradford, and in rare times of very heavy rain there is too much water for the river to carry and the streets are flooded.

The 'lost' rivers of London flow underground. These are the West-bourne, Tyburn, Effra and Fleet. All these rivers have 'above ground' names to commemorate them. Do you know where they are?

Have you ever been at the seaside when there has been a high tide? Have you watched the big waves rolling in from the sea and lashing

The Severn Bore

against the promenade? On some
rivers at certain times of the year a
high tide such as this rolls up the
river. The water already in the
river is not able to absorb all this sea
water. So, for miles and miles a sort
of wall of water travels up the river.
This is known as a **bore**. Not all
rivers have bores. Those that do are
the Severn, the Trent, the Wye and
the Solway.

A bore always comes from the sea
into the river estuary and then up the
river. It does not start inland. Bores
are very interesting and in some cases
the ridge of water reaches several
feet in height. If you live, or are
staying, near a river that has a bore,
the local newspaper will tell you the
time it is expected to arrive.

7 River life

1 Mammals

Not many of the wild animals in Britain live in the water. All the same you will probably see animals in or near a river. Some go there to drink or swim, some to escape from an enemy. They seem to know that water will make them lose their scent.

The otter

He hunts for food at night. He has a broad flat head, a short face, bright black eyes and small rounded ears. Notice his tapering tail that acts as a rudder when he swims. He has short strong legs with webbed feet enabling him to swim. Otters swim under water but must come to the surface to breathe. They have two layers of fur that prevent them getting cold. The under layer is soft, whitish, grey fur with brown tips. This is covered by longer, coarser hairs – grey at the base becoming a rich brown. When he is out of the water an otter looks glossy and brown. Otters live in large holes in the river bank sheltered and hidden by overhanging leaves and grass.

The water vole

He is about twelve inches long from nose tip to tail tip and has a blunt round nose and a long tail. His fur is reddish brown and thick and glossy. Some of the water voles that live in Scotland and eastern England have black fur. He lives in a burrow in the river bank. The water vole is sometimes called a water rat.

The water shrew

A smaller animal is the water shrew, about three or four inches long. He has a fat little body with a long tail. He can be seen swimming along near the surface of the water and not far from the bank as he tries to catch insects. Under water he has a silvery appearance but on the bank you will see that his fur is white on his underside and dark brown on top.

2 Amphibians
The frog

A cold-blooded creature that begins life as a tadpole with gills. Later on it develops lungs and can live on dry land. It has very powerful hind legs that enable it to leap.

Toads and newts are also amphibians.

3 Insects
The mayfly

This, as its name suggests, can be seen on warm May days. It has four

DRAGONFLY

FRESHWATER SHRIMP

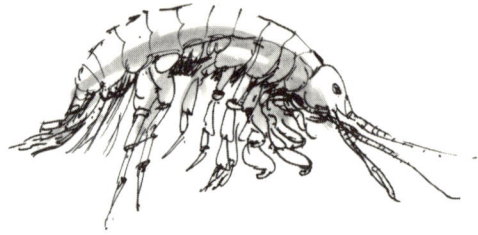

OTTER

WATER SHREW

WATER VOLE

COMMON FROG & TADPOLE

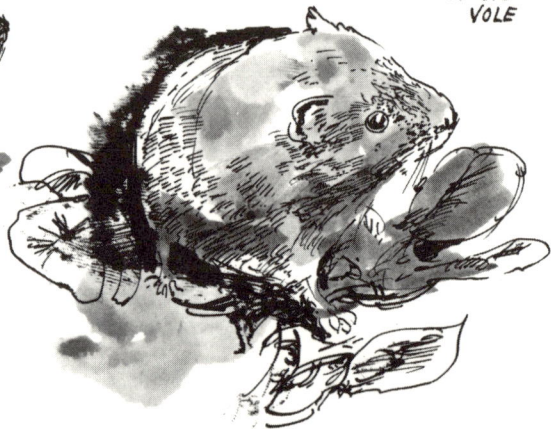

very fine and delicate wings, the fore wings longer than the hind wings. It has a slender body and at the end are three long very fine threads like tails. When it has become an adult the mayfly rarely lives longer than a day or perhaps two days at the most.

The caddis fly

This is rather like a moth and can be seen in the evening flying about by the weeds and bushes at the riverside. During the day it spends its time sitting on the boughs of trees and stems of plants. It has brown hairy wings, the forewings longer and narrower than the hind. It has longish legs and feelers or antennae.

The dragonfly

Another freshwater insect that is worth watching out for is the dragonfly with its brilliant body colouring and shining wings. Dragonflies are carnivorous, eating large numbers of insects.

Find out as much as you can about insects – how they hatch and grow and what the various stages of development are called.

4 Crustaceans

A large group of creatures that includes crabs, lobsters, crayfish and shrimps. The word 'crustacean' comes from the Latin *crusta* meaning 'shell', so all these creatures have hard shells.

The freshwater shrimp

Very common in streams and rivers all over Great Britain. They are about three-quarters of an inch long and scud about very quickly. If you push over a stone by the river's edge. you are likely to see a lot.

The freshwater crayfish

This looks very much like a lobster but is only about four inches long. Crayfish are nocturnal, living under stones and in burrows during the day, so you will be very lucky if you see one.

5 Fish
The salmon

Perhaps you will be lucky enough to see fish leap up the river. Salmon and trout are the two types of fish that do this, but as we will see, many of our rivers are now too polluted for salmon and trout to live there. A male salmon is a greenish colour at the top and a pinkish colour at the bottom with many spots on its upper part. The female is a silvery purple colour and her back is tinged with green. Her body too has many spots. The salmon leaps up waterfalls so that it can get upstream to lay its eggs. It is prepared to make this long and tiring journey in order to find a place where it can leave its eggs in peace and safety.

The young salmon stay in the river for several years and then migrate to the sea where they stay for several more years. Only then are they ready to return to freshwater to lay their eggs. By some incredible biological compass they manage to return to the same river where they grew up.

The trout
The colour of a trout varies according to the type of river or stream in which it lives. It may be green or gold, orange or a steely colour. Like the salmon (it belongs to the same family) it has spots on its body. It too swims and leaps upstream to lay its eggs.

The perch
A full grown perch is dark olive green in colour shading to a golden brown. Across his back are broad dark bars.

The minnow
This is a small fish with a short blunt nose. It has a large forked tail and is dark brownish green on the back with dark bars. The underside is silvery. The colours change according to the season.

The pike
A yellowish or greenish fish with a flat snout. It can grow up to a length of three feet or more and has a long life span. They are to be found in lakes and slow-moving rivers where they lie in wait, motionless, for their prey. Their colouring is a good camouflage.

The tench
Dark brown or green body with a thick and slimy skin. When mature the fish measures about a foot. Lives in lakes, ponds, and slow-flowing rivers, and feeds on larvae and snails.

The carp
Golden yellow in colour, the carp lives in stagnant or very slow-moving water with dense vegetation. It is intensively 'farmed' in commercial carp-ponds in southern and eastern Europe.

6 Plants
Comfrey
Grows in watery places. Its flower varies from a dull white or yellow to dull pink or purple. It is rather a juicy plant and might not be easy to press. It has also the names All Heal and Boneset. The pulp was squeezed over a broken bone, where it set firmly. Eaten raw it is still used by gipsies as a cure for gastric ulcers.

Marsh marigold or kingcup
This is a common plant that grows in wet places – marshy meadows and margins of streams. It is about 6–12 inches high and flowers in April–June.

Water cress
In midstream you may see water cress growing in dense green masses. Its leaves are eaten as salad.

Yellow flag
This grows in shallow water; the flowers are bright yellow and can be seen from a distance. When they saw it afar travellers knew that they were approaching a place where they could easily cross the river.

SALMON

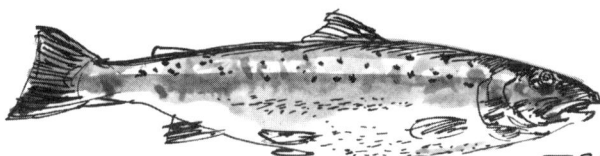

TROUT

PIKE

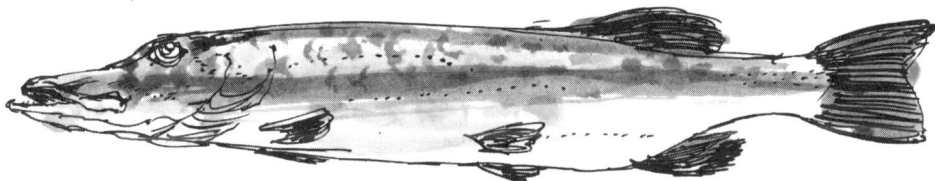

TENCH

CARP

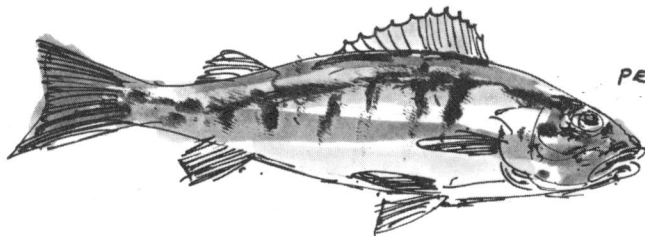

PERCH

REEDMACE

BULRUSH

YELLOW FLAG

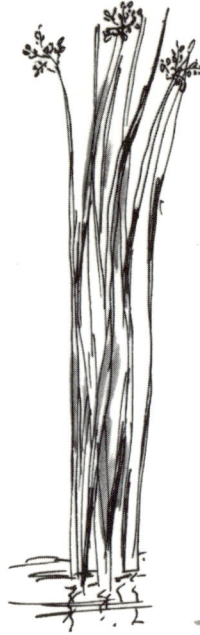

REED

WATER CRESS

MARSH MARIGOLD

KINGFISHER

GREY HERON

MOORHEN

COOT

MALLARD

MUTE SWAN

DIPPER

Reed

Particularly common in Norfolk around lakes, rivers and marshes, reeds led to the big thatching industry in that county. Reeds were also used to stuff hassocks (church kneelers) and for upholstery.

Bulrush

Grows in slow-flowing water and in lakes. It was used for rush lights in the Middle Ages and after. Pick one and starting at the bottom split the green rind and run your thumbnail along the white pith. It was the white pith that was soaked in grease, dried and then used as a light.

Reedmace

This was sometimes used as a torch. It was soaked in oil but gave rather a smoky flame. The fibres of the leaves can be used for ropes and textiles.

7 Birds
The swan

The swan that you are most likely to see is called the mute swan. It has an orange bill with a black knob. It is usually silent (hence the name) but hisses when it gets annoyed.

The kingfisher

You may be lucky enough to see a kingfisher perching on a branch over-hanging the water and diving to catch fish. It likes slow-moving water and nests in burrows in the river bank.

The heron

A wading bird, the heron is grey with white head and neck and black crest. Feeds in shallow or coastal water and you might see it standing very still, waiting to catch fish. It nests in trees.

The dipper

Not found in southern or eastern England. It likes fast streams in hills and mountains and you might see it bobbing about on rocks in midstream. It can swim both on the water and under it and even walks on the stream bed.

The mallard

Feeds on the surface of the water by upending itself. The drake (male) has a dark green head, narrow white collar, purple brown breast and grey body. The duck (female) is brown.

The moorhen

Often confused with coots. It has a red forehead, white line along flank and can be seen in town parks.

The coot

Black all over but with a striking white forehead.

8 Water, water

We have seen that water is very important: industries grew up near rivers, water was used for power. But water itself is so precious an element in life – any life – that no living creature, animal or vegetable can exist without it. Those who go on hunger strike can live for many weeks without food. But if they are deprived of water they will soon die.

During a long period of drought **water diviners** were sometimes

The source of the Thames at Thames Head in the Cotswolds. In 1958 the Thames Conservancy placed a statue of Father Thames here, but because the spring is so often dry many people believe that the true source of the Thames is at Seven Springs near Cheltenham

used to find new places in the earth where wells could be sunk and water found. The word diviner comes from the Latin word *divinare* meaning to foretell. The most usual way of water divining was to use a divining rod – a long forked branch or twig of hazel. This was held between the finger and thumb and turned itself when held near the earth over any hidden treasure such as precious metals or a spring.

Wells, where fresh water was obtained, were usually treated with respect. The most important were dedicated to a saint: many have stories about them. At Wavertree, near Liverpool is a well with a Latin inscription which translated means 'who giveth not what he hath, the devil below, seeth'. Travellers, when they had had a drink to refresh themselves, left alms (money for the poor) there. If they did not do this a devil supposed to be chained at the bottom of the well, laughed. Monks in a nearby monastery received the financial contributions.

At Brislington, near Bristol it is the custom on July 25 the eve of the feast of St Anne for the clergy and parishioners of St Anne's Church, Brislington, to make a pilgrimage to St Anne's well. St Anne is the patroness of harbours, ports and sailors. As early as the fifteenth century processions were made to the well whose water was supposed to have healing powers. Pilgrimages have not been

made continuously since the fifteenth century. For many years the well has been in ruins. It was acquired in 1924 by the Corporation who repaired it and have cared for it since.

In Derbyshire in many villages there is the quaint and colourful custom of **well dressing**. This takes place each year although the date differs from village to village. At Tissington, perhaps the most well known 'well dressing' village, the five wells are dressed on Ascension Day. There are two stories associated with this. One is that during the Black Death, a plague which struck Britain between 1348 and 1349, seventy-seven out of a hundred Derbyshire priests died. Tissington escaped without a single death because of the purity of its springs. The other story is that in 1615 there was a very long drought and throughout the time the springs of Tissington continued to flow and people came from all over the district to get water. Whichever story is true obviously the villagers like to give thanks to God for His gift of water.

Work begins in Tissington weeks before Ascension Day. The leader of each team – the five wells are each dressed by a different team – selects a text from the Bible and draws on paper a picture to illustrate it. This is

A roadside well near Longparish in Hampshire (opposite)

enlarged and an outline copied onto clay to form the basis of the picture. Peas, beans, maize, berries, petals of wild and cultivated flowers, mosses, grasses and stones are used to decorate the picture. The result is very beautiful and colourful.

At Barlow the well dressing is held on the Wednesday after St Laurence's Day (August 10). At Youlgreave the village communal taps are dressed on the Saturday nearest to St John the Baptist's Day (June 24).

Evil spirits too were associated with springs and rivers. At Waddow Hall in Lancashire is a well, 'Peggy's Well', whose evil spirit Peggy, was blamed for all mishaps. If a cow was sick, a chicken stolen, a sheep strayed or a child ill, this, and any other calamity was said to be her responsibility. The River Ure, near Middleham in Yorkshire is said to have a kelpie or river horse. It is said that this claims one human victim each year.

During the eighteenth century it became fashionable to 'take the waters'. Some spring water has certain minerals dissolved in it such as salt, iron and sulphur. This of course depends on the type of rock in the district. People were sure that such water was good for curing rheumatism and similar aches and pains. They believed that to drink it or bathe in it was of benefit. It was soon found that in districts in which such supplies of

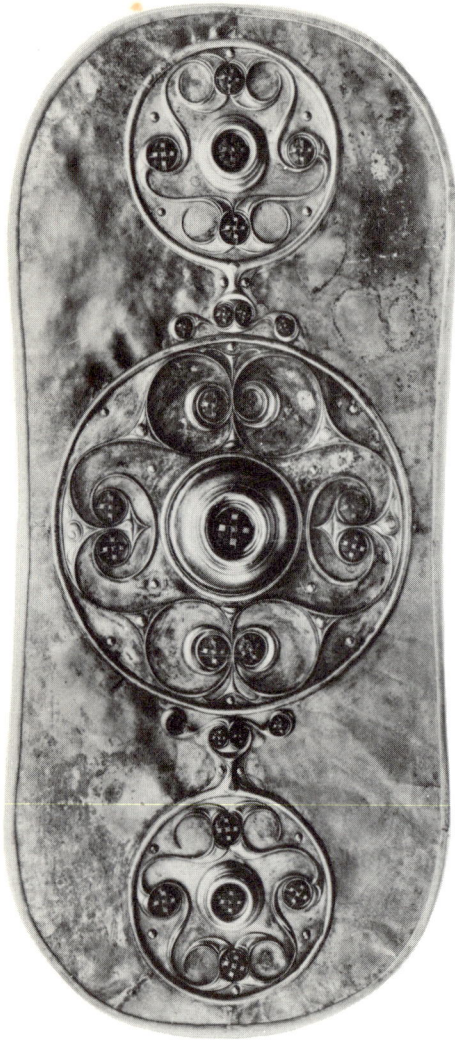

Bronze shield (first century AD) found in the Thames. It is believed that the Britons (and later the Romans) threw coins and weapons into rivers to placate the river gods (By courtesy of the British Museum)

Bath Spa

water were plentiful a profitable
business could grow running lodging
houses for those who came to take the
waters. Towns developed near the
springs and to them came people
seeking cures for their ailments. These
towns were known as Spas. No doubt
many who came were sufferers in
great pain. But visiting spas was
fashionable in the eighteenth century
and many wealthy people came
simply because it was the fashionable
thing to do. Spa towns are Scar-
borough, Tunbridge Wells, Bath and
Harrogate.

9 Pollution

You will notice that in the later section of the river the water does not sparkle as it does in the early section. It is cloudy and dirty and probably smells. This is because it is polluted by factories that send their waste into it, by some 'battery' farmers who send in manure, and by sewage. Pollution is a great problem. Many English rivers are very dirty, so much so that fish can no longer live there. No fish can live in water that contains less than 3.3 parts of oxygen to a million parts of water. One Midland river is so polluted that not even the loglouse and the bloodworm, which are the lowest forms of river creatures, can live there.

Detergent foam on the river

The Trent, the Thames and the Tyne were once fine rivers for salmon. In the 1870s the Tyne produced 130,000 salmon per year. Now it produces very few. There are none in the Trent and the Thames.

Acts of Parliament have given the twenty-nine River Authorities powers to stop factories sending harmful waste into rivers. But not enough has been done about this. Not enough has been done to make the public aware of the seriousness of the problem of polluted rivers. In 1974 ten Water Authorities are to be set up. They will replace the existing River Authorities and will be responsible, among other things, for preventing river pollution. It is essential that this should be done. For one thing those who depend on salmon fishing for a living need clean water. Many more people now go into the countryside at weekends. They want to paddle, bathe and sail boats on rivers. They too need clean water.

It is not easy for children by themselves to find out the amount of pollution in a river. In any case it could be dangerous. An official taking a sample from a river burnt his hand as the water was so full of acid. Other rivers are polluted with deadly poisons such as cyanide. Some schools work on this problem as a school project. Perhaps you could ask your teacher to write to your local River Authority (or after 1974, Water Authority), to find out about this. You, by yourself, or with other members of your class can tell people about the seriousness of the problem, you can write a letter to your local newspaper or your local councillor or your member of parliament.

Perhaps you were one of the 15,000 schoolchildren who took part in a survey of Britain's streams and rivers, organized by the Advisory Centre for Education. This survey found that our rivers are indeed polluted, but that some are getting better. In conjunction with *The Sunday Times*, the Centre is starting a children's club, 'Watch', that will concern itself with all aspects of the environment – rivers, air, trees, noise, etc.

The River Authorities of
England and Wales

10 Things to do

No doubt you will not be content for long just to look at your river. Most people like to collect things. One of the cheapest and easiest things to collect is information. Make a scrapbook of rivers. Look through magazines and newspapers for scraps of information. These need not be pieces of news. You might find photographs, poems or odd facts (for example which is the longest river in Europe). Keep a notebook near you. Jot down any facts you hear on the radio or T.V.

Make a scrap book of your own river. How many different sorts of bridges cross it? Is there still a bridge that is owned by a person or a group of people and for which a fee, or toll, is charged when one crosses? If you can find one near your home visit it. Spend a few minutes watching traffic crossing. Does the collection of tolls delay traffic?

If you travel along, or across a river, or part of a river by boat or ferry, use your camera to record what you see. Many rivers, for example the Tyne, Mersey and Tame, flow through industrial areas. Here there are many houses and factories. But not all parts

of England are industrial. You will possibly visit a river that flows through beautiful countryside, for example the river Dart. Photographs of rivers will enable you to compare and contrast.

Make drawings too. How is your river used? Are there rowing boats on it? Are canoe slaloms organised there?

Until the end of the eighteenth century when James Watt improved the steam engine all factories depended on water for power. To find out how swiftly water flowed farmers and millers used a rough and ready method of floating a piece of wood down the river. This they did several times and took the average speed. Try this. See how many you can count as your wood races downstream. Is there any difference in speed between wood sent at the edge of the river and that in the middle?

We read earlier that workers in the woollen industry needed soft water. Test your river water for softness. Scoop water from the river in a jam jar. Be careful not to fall in. Into your jam jar put several drops of washing-up liquid. Shake or stir the water. If it lathers easily it is soft water.

Collect pebbles from the side of the river. If you spend some time looking at them you will see that some have rather pretty markings. You will see too that there are several different sorts of stone. Take some home, wash and polish them. Perhaps your school has a tumbling machine for polishing stones. Or you may know someone who owns one who would let you see, or even use it. You could use one of the smaller stones to weight paper down so that it does not blow away. Perhaps you could use one of the bigger ones to hold a door open, or several bigger ones as part of a rockery in the garden.

If you have more time and patience you can collect wild flowers. Remember that flowers grow naturally in the countryside. They are there because nature put them there for people to enjoy. You may pick them, although it is not advisable to pick too many, but you may *NOT* uproot them. See how many different sorts you can find.

If you want to press these flowers pick only one of each. But be sure to get a leaf. When you have pressed the flowers you can stick them into a notebook. Remember to put at the top of the page the date on which you found them, and the place. In addition to the name of the place it is a good idea to put the type of place, such as moorland, meadow, or riverside. Your wanderings may take you away from rivers.

You can press flowers between sheets of clean blotting paper or kitchen paper. Be sure to spread them out well and see that the petals and leaves are flat. When you have done this put another sheet of paper on top. Then lift this onto thick newspaper (a whole one). On top of this put something very heavy, such as a pile of large books. As you must leave them for a week, be sure that they are in a place which is out of people's way.

Rivers have inspired many people. Smetana, a Czechoslovakian musician, wrote a piece of music describing the adventures of a river as it travelled on its way. It is called 'Vltava'. Part of this music makes the river dance as it travels joyfully past a village wedding. Perhaps on your recorder you could play dancing notes for a happy river and slow, long, sad ones for a polluted river. Even if you cannot manage to play a tune you could make the rhythm. There is a beautiful song called 'The Waters of Tyne' about this big river in the North of England. Can you think of any more songs or pieces of music about rivers?

It may be that you are more interested in words than music. William Wordsworth, a famous English poet, wrote poems about the River Duddon in the English Lake District. Why not write a poem about your own river?

Do you remember Tom in *The Water Babies*? When he wrote this book Charles Kingsley was staying at a house not far from the water sinks we mentioned in Chapter 5. If you look at the picture of Malham Cove, you will see a black mark down the front. This is a natural discolouration of the rock. Charles Kingsley pretended that it was the sooty mark made by Tom when he escaped from his master and slid down the limestone cliff. The stream at the bottom where he landed is where he joined the Water Babies. Of course all this is imaginary. Perhaps you can write a story using your imagination. The good thing about imaginary stories is that no one can say they are wrong.

Possibly the ships, cranes and buoys in the river mouth interest you more. Can you watch the cranes hoisting goods on to ships? How many ships still have hoist lifts for cars? How many have drive-on car ferries? If you have a tape recorder perhaps you can interview people who are travelling to and from overseas. Or you could talk to those who load and unload cargo. Remember not to ask them when they are very busy. Remember too to keep well out of the way of moving cranes. They are dangerous. Of course you know that you must be polite.

Keep a nature diary of part of the bank of your local river. Keep it for a whole year. Notice the different wild flowers and birds that come in the different seasons. Have you ever rubbed a soft pencil over paper with a coin underneath? You will have got an impression of the coin on the paper. You can rub leaves or tree bark in the same way. You will need a large piece of white paper, shelf or ceiling or lining paper will be suitable as long as it is not too thin. Fasten this to the tree with Sellotape. Rub it with heel ball. (Heel ball is cobblers' wax.) You will have to ask a shoe-mender for it, but you will possibly find that it is rather difficult to get. If you cannot get any use a black wax crayon, the thicker the better.

The oldest rocks in the British Isles were made about 800 million years ago. Those at Malham, the scene of *The Water Babies* about 350 million years ago. If you draw a time-chart in your note book using a scale of 1 inch to represent 1000 years you will find that you are easily able to show the years from 3000 BC (when the New Stone Age Men came) to 1973. It will take 5 inches. How long would your time-chart have to be to show 800 million years? The answer will surprise you. You certainly will not be able to fit this in your book. If we decide that 1 millimetre will represent 1000 years how long will the scale be then? How much space will represent one year?

Many of your activities will take you
very near rivers. You will be tempted
perhaps to paddle, swim or even take
a boat onto the river. This *can* be
dangerous even though it may look
safe. Tragedies are caused each
summer by children who swim and
boat on dangerous stretches of river.
Small children who cannot swim
sometimes fall in. If you are a
swimmer you will be familiar with
the handbook of the Royal Life
Saving Society. This stresses the fact
that if you cannot swim well it is
better to run to fetch help if you see
someone in trouble, rather than try
yourself to rescue them. If you jump
in it is possible that you too will
drown. Do remember that a person
who is drowning will struggle and you
will find a struggling person difficult
to deal with. So in case of accident
get help as quickly as possible.
Here is a verse to remind you that *all*
rivers can be dangerous:

Says Tweed tae Till
'What gars ye rin sae still?'
Says Till tae Tweed
'Though ye rin wi' speed
And I rin slaw,
For ae man ye droon
I droon twa.'

11 Books

Rivers

M O Greenwood	*Discovering Rivers*
N & M Muller	*The Junior True Book of Rivers*
Ede Maré	*London's River*
P Rondière	*Water*
J Murphy & C Keeping	*How They Were Built – Dams*
F Wilkins	*Bridges in Britain*

Surnames

	How did we get our names?
Ray Bethers	*The story of surnames*
Lilian Devereux	*How surnames began*
C M Matthews	*Your book of surnames*
Pennethorne Hughes	*Is thy name Wart?*

Nature

	Wild flowers of the countryside
A J Huxley	*Wild flowers*
W R Philipson	*Your book of wild flowers*
Miles Hadfield	*A first book of wild flowers*
Joan Dean	*British Wild Flowers*
Ladybird Series	*Birds of Britain*
Wilfred Willett	*Your book of Bird watching*
Miles Hadfield	*Birds and their lives*
Alison Ross	*Pond and River birds*
Ladybird Series	*Sea and Estuary Birds*
	Book of trees
	British Trees
C A Hall and B A Jay	*Your book of trees*
Miles Hadfield	*What to look for in Spring*
Ladybird Series	*What to look for in Summer*
	What to look for in Autumn
	What to look for in Winter